Happiness in Your Life - Book Two: Intuition

Doe Zantamata

DEDICATION

For my Mom.

CONTENTS

ACKNOWLEDGMENTS

Thank you to all those who have been with me on this journey, even if just for a little while. Thank you to you who is reading this book for our connection within these pages and beyond.

1 THE SENSE

Intuition is a sense, just like sight, touch, or any of your other senses. There's really no magic to it. You have it naturally, and you can either train it to be able to better use it, or not. It, like all your other senses, was given to you to help you navigate through life. Some people call it their "gut feeling" and others refer to it only as their conscience or a knowing...it's all pretty much the same. It's that feeling inside that tells you right or wrong, yes or no.

Some people have a stronger natural sense of intuition, just like some people are born with incredible hearing. Some people take the time to train their intuition, as most of us were trained to use our other senses when we were children. Hearing uses sound, sight uses three-dimensional images, and intuition uses the energy of emotion. Training and using your intuition is as valuable as using any other sense and without it, you're missing part of the world.

When you were little, through a billion questions, you learned what all the sights, sounds, tastes, and smells in the world around you were. Fluffy beings were labeled dogs, cats, hamsters, and bunnies. Sounds were labeled the vacuum cleaner, coffee maker, car starting, and so on. You were a constant sponge and learned so much, but likely you weren't ever taught to pay attention to the signals being given to you by your intuition.

Intuition literally means learning from within. Become aware of and learn to trust your inner feeling and it will become stronger. Avoid going against your better judgment or getting talked into things that just don't feel right.

Intuition most often is a sense that gives you a present feeling of future consequences. This isn't psychic. You've seen lightning with your eyes countless times and only after a few seconds do you hear the sound it makes, thunder. This does not mean you are psychic if you see lightning and announce, "Soon there will be thunder." Everyone knows it. At some point you didn't know it but were taught, and since then, you take it as a given that it's going to happen every time. And it does.

As you learn to trust and act on your sense of intuition, it will continue to strengthen. Sooner or later, it will become like any other sense, and will guide you toward good and away from danger. If you saw a train coming toward you, you would move away from it. If you hear the phone ring, you answer it. This will become the way your intuition works. You will "just know" when to move toward or away from people and circumstances as reliably as if you saw, heard, or knew with information from any other sense.

If it's a sense and it is so helpful, WHY ON EARTH wouldn't you be taught how to use it?

The simple answer is, because your parents weren't. And their parents weren't. A person can only give what they have, so this missing giant hunk of knowledge has eluded generation upon generation.

Bizarre, isn't it?

Not really. Think about history versus now. We live in a patriarchal society, meaning it's mostly been men in charge and masculine energy ruling the world. Intuition is stronger in women because women are more in touch with their feelings and are allowed by society to develop and use them more in childhood and adulthood. Men aren't. For thousands of years we've been in battles over territory and resources and it was necessary to survive to rely mostly on brawn and the physically strongest were the ones who would survive. So in order to kill people or take all their stuff, it was also necessary to shut down feelings and conscience or die. Nowadays, yes there are still wars. But in many places, there is peace and has been for a few decades at least. So many of us can safely go from survival mode to thriving mode, or…natural. It's not natural to be at war. It's not natural to ignore your constant stream of feelings. The modes of operation that are perfectly normal during war in order for the person to survive are totally abnormal after war and wreck what could be a good life. It is totally possible to switch gears and shift into thriving mode. Using your feelings and intuition are a huge part of that switch. Your life will change enormously for the better. Your inner peace will become seeded, take root, and develop and strengthen over time with patience and practice.

Sound good? I hope so, otherwise the rest of this book is going to be bo'ring.

Some folks may wonder if using intuition is against their religion. Let's clear that up right here and now.

Intuition in The Bible:

Who gives intuition to the heart and instinct to the mind?

-Job 38:36 NLT

Intuition in the Qur'an:

17:36 And do not uphold what you have no knowledge of. For the hearing, eyesight, <u>and heart</u>, all these you are responsible for.

Intuition in the Dhammapada (Buddhism):
...a rightly directed mind brings greater good than any relative or friend (vv. 42-43)

s. "The Living Message of the Dhammapada", by Bhikkhu Bodhi. *Access to Insight (Legacy Edition)*, 5 June, 2010.

If you are not religious, it's a sense, biologically a part of you. If you are religious, it's a sense, given to you to use just like all of your other senses.

So let's use it.

When you start to train your intuition, you'll likely not be perfect at it. Just the same as when you were starting to train your mind to recognize your other senses. You may mistake a signal for something else, or you may miss some things entirely. Don't feel foolish or like this intuition thing is fake. It's not. You've never thought your sense of hearing was fake just because you could have sworn you heard a knock at the door but when you looked there was no one there. So if you thought your intuition was moving you towards something good but it didn't turn out to be anything, don't give up on your intuition because of that or think you shouldn't pay it any mind.

It could be that you already feel like you have a strong sense of intuition and have been using it without really much knowledge of it, but still using it quite a lot. Everyone has different strengths of all senses. As you consciously train it, you'll be able to discern very subtle differences, eventually almost automatically, just the same as a sommelier can discern different flavors in wine versus a person having a sip for the first time and only being able to tell if they like it or not.

Even just recognizing intuition as a sense will help you heaps. In its most basic form, it will tell you if you're going to benefit from an experience or not. Your mind isn't the enemy. Your mind is supposed to be just a processor of all the senses and it does a great job at that.

Most people trust their senses all the time except intuition and don't tend to argue with them. If you smell the milk and it smells rotten, you'll likely trust your nose without having to drink the milk and get sick from it. You don't need the milk to prove it to you. Yet so many people have a distinct bad feeling about something and then get talked into doing it anyway, going anyway, only to regret it later on. How many times have you thought, "I knew something wasn't right about this!" or "I had a feeling this wasn't going to be good!" In those cases, your intuition was screaming at you beforehand but you forced yourself to ignore it and found out later what it was trying to say. Then those circumstances proved to you what your intuition knew all along.

You have to be confident in your intuition or it may end up being more frustrating than if you didn't have the sense at all. But confidence doesn't mean not listening to what anyone else has to say, ever. It means certainty of how you feel but still being open to what to do. It means knowing what's right for you, just like if your sense of taste told you that you didn't like babaganoush you wouldn't eat a whole plate of it no matter if a whole room full of people loved the stuff. You have to do what's right for you in life, not what's popular or what another person really, really wants even though you really, really don't.

Now at this point in life, if you've never consciously used it, it is more difficult and takes longer to train your intuition than it would had you learned it as a child along with your other senses. Also at this point in life, you've seen a lot of faces, heard a lot of voices, and you've been hurt, let down, rejected, and deceived. So you've got some baggage. We all do. In the beginning, it's important to step back when you have a bad feeling about something important and reflect on if this is really your intuition speaking to you or if it's a traumatic memory that hasn't fully healed coming through as fear. When your intuition discourages something, it doesn't come through as fear. It comes through as distaste, annoyance, or even repulsion on some level…just a feeling that this isn't something you like or want. Again think of your other senses. If you taste a food that you don't like, you don't feel scared of it⁓you just don't like it.

Intuition won't prevent you from all painful experiences, no matter how well trained you've got it. There are some things that are just unseen at first glance and must be lived through as lessons. These are often very painful but always important lessons. To avoid them completely would mean avoiding emotional growth and though it may not seem so at the time, it actually wouldn't be a good thing to skip them. Your intuition is never your enemy. If it drew you to an emotionally painful experience, especially one that was reminiscent of your childhood life, it was to have you grow through it and release it. It may be that you expressed a desire to be free of a limitation or to remove a block to and increase your self worth. Your intuition will get you there, but sometimes the road to the beautiful destination is muddy and full of obstacles and potholes. As the saying goes, you can't have the rainbow without the rain. Once the limitation or block is released, however, you're free. You won't have to live that again. Most of these come in the form of romantic relationships. You may have been very drawn to a person upon first meeting who turned out later to be a jerk. But what you learned about yourself, your value, what you deserve, and who you are, you couldn't have had if you hadn't had that relationship or one very similar to it. Those are the hidden gifts.

Sometimes when we look back we cherry pick experiences and wish we could take some but leave others. Even regretting the ones we would rather not have had without considering that without those, there's no way we could have had the good ones that happened, too. For example a horrible marriage that produced beautiful children. Wanting to go back and never be with that spouse would mean those children would have never been born. Emphasize your focus on internal gratitude for the gifts and the pain will lessen over time and with acceptance that the past can't be changed anyway. In the future, you won't be drawn to that again, but looking to the past, you can be grateful that you made it through and are wiser today for the experience.

In those difficult but important learning times, your intuition won't steer you completely away from them but it will help guide you through them in the best way possible.

This author actually had a major car accident that led to one of the best friendships she ever had in her life. Had it not been for the "unfortunate" accident, that incredible friendship would have been missed entirely.

Your intuition is real, it's amazingly helpful, and it will be very beneficial to become fully aware of it and use it in daily life.

2 USING INTUITION DAILY

A lot of times when people talk about intuition, they talk about huge, momentous things like "I had a feeling I shouldn't go on that airplane. And then it crashed." But that really doesn't happen much. The best benefits of intuition are found in the same places as your other senses; the hundreds of tiny, everyday things that can either be smooth or difficult.

Intuition alone won't help you to have smooth sailing throughout the little things of the day. You have to also believe in good things, believe those good things can happen to you, and believe you deserve them. Belief drives reality. If you believe yourself to be unlucky, then your intuition can't give you the lucky things that would be open to you if you believed you were lucky. It's a conflict, and your beliefs will always win. If the odd lucky thing happened to sneak by, your belief system would either dismiss it or ruin it.

Now, you don't have to have all your self-worth bits worked out or be 100% confident and secure before you can have good things happen. Think of it not as why would good things happen to you, but why wouldn't they? Good things happen to everyone, including jerks! Welcome the good things with appreciation and more will show up or be noticed in your life. That is a promise.

Some ways you can use everyday intuition:

- Deciding which route to drive to a place

- Deciding which movie or restaurant to visit

- Thinking of a friend "out of the blue" and deciding to give them a call to say hi

- Needing to purchase something and taking a pause before deciding which store to get it from. Your intuition can help direct you to a sale or good price —don't knock it until you try it…you'll be pleasantly surprised!

- Finding a good place to park

- Creating a peaceful space in your mind via meditation

Again this isn't some kind of psychic bologna…it's just making use of your sense and still using your brain to process it. Don't feel silly or naïve for trying it. You'll actually find it works amazingly well and you'll wonder why not everyone knows about it or uses it, too!

You may also think that it seems a little odd to be mentally talking to yourself throughout the day, but you actually already do...you just may not be aware of it. At any given point, you have thoughts going through your mind at lightning speed and making subconscious decisions for you about what you are doing, who you are, and who other people are around you. So you can either pay attention and direct a few of these millions of thoughts, or ignore them and let them run your life based on unawareness and subconscious reactions...which is what most people do on a daily basis.

One important thing to note is that you don't have to prove this to anyone. You shouldn't really push anyone to try to do the same as you because their belief system may just not be ready for it (and may never be). Instead of being grateful and having their life improve, they may think you've lost your mind and that they are the ones living in reality. If a person is convinced that reality is boring or difficult, there's not much you can do to change their beliefs. They've likely been really disappointed or hurt and subconsciously think they are somehow protecting themselves by not believing in any good things anymore. All they are really doing, however, is living a life that's constantly disappointing instead of only sometimes.

Intuition and Creativity

One of the most amazing and magical ways of using intuition is with creativity. The art of thinking less and really enjoying and being in the moment of creative flow is a very personal but wholly fulfilling use of time.

There are many very famous artists, singers, songwriters, inventors, and authors who set their

DOE ZANTAMATA

mind on their work, allow their mind to be in a receptive space, do it, and really enjoy it. Something opens up in them in which ideas, melodies, entire songs or books aren't thought up but rather appear in their mind. Almost like a whisper in their ear. This is fully realized creative intuition. It's a real gift and is very special.

Allowing yourself to be in that creative space and making time to be there is a form of meditation and will increase your intuition. It's a place of peace, non-judgment, and openness. Even cooking, scrapbooking, redecorating a bathroom, rebuilding an old classic car, or making homemade soap can be a creative, meditative process.

You put pure, beautiful energy in and the live in the creative moment, not stuck on how it's going to turn out exactly but with a goal in mind. Solutions along the way aren't thought about really hard and

20

calculated, worked out with loads of math or complex thinking...they are brilliant in hindsight but when in that space, ideas for certain things just "come to you." They arrive easily to a welcoming mind. That's why it's so fun and such a gift, literally. It also teaches you that you have to be doing in order to receive them. This encourages you to do more to improve and to live more often in that place of connection.

Upon completion of projects made there, there's a great feeling of joy and accomplishment. It's a different kind of joy that can only be accomplished through allowing this creative zone to live through you because an experience of freedom and connection live in that work.

And again, it can be really good banana bread... it doesn't have to be the Sistine Chapel. Pure creation is a freedom of mind and a dance with the energetic field where you get to leave all your thoughts, worries, and problems for a little while.

Plus you make great stuff.

What is creative intuition, exactly? Well, that's open to interpretation and depends on your beliefs. To many, it's Divinely inspired work. The feeling of something incredibly unique that shows up and comes through you.

Does it really matter exactly who or where or why it comes?

Could it just be absolute creativity experienced when you allow yourself to be fully immersed in the moment? Yes...could be.

Could it be a gift from a lost loved one who has turned into a guardian angel, supporting and encouraging you to do what you love? Maybe.

Could it be a direct message from God? Could be.

Could it be something "evil?" Doubt it.

It doesn't follow with the feelings. The feelings that come with it are love and gratitude. Evil, or bad feelings have only temporary pleasure or power but guilt or uncertainty follow afterwards.

In this way, intuition helps recognize intuition. If it feels right, good, honest, pure, and with appreciation, it's based out of love, wherever the source.

Intuition and Decision Making

You can never make a full decision on only a little information. But most times, all the information's not all readily right there for you to see. This is where intuition helps a lot. If you're feeling a lot of hesitation but logically an idea sounds fine, then it may not be something to dive into. If you're feeling drawn to it, then either it's the right thing or there's a lesson in it that a part of you wants to learn. In uncertainty, stay very aware of your feelings throughout the day. If the feelings are more heavy than expansive, it may be something you let go of without having to find out what those feelings were indicating early on. If you have a lot of really good feelings inside even though doubts may enter your mind later, then going with it is probably a much better road to follow. Let your intuition be your guide, but keep your mind alert to process what it is telling you.

Intuition and Intention Setting

A mind that doesn't meditate is like an ocean in the middle of a storm. Big waves of thoughts swirling about, crashing into each other and so many things going on it's hard to pay attention to any one long enough before it disappears. Now imagine a very still lake. That's the goal of meditation. If you were to drop a rock in that swirling ocean, you couldn't even tell where it went or if it made any effect. But if you were to drop that same rock in the still lake, you'd be able to see the ripples moving outward from where it was dropped and focus on that one area easily. A mind on meditation has clarity, calm, and is able to hold and process a thought and to allow other thoughts to come in and be noticed. Intention setting is similar to goal setting except there's no fixed end date or rigid expected outcome. In a clear, calm mind, the intention is that rock. By meditating on it and allowing it to ripple out naturally, your mind will be fed with amazing insights and ideas that will seem to just show up out of nowhere.

Intuition and Honesty

Even if the best liars in the world can never fool themselves. Intuition follows truth in the form of conscience. Some people think they're able to numb or relieve their weighted conscience to a certain extent by justifying dishonest or deceitful behavior, and on their mind level, they may be able to argue to others as to why they were "right" in cheating in a committed relationship, skimming money from a business they work for or from their taxes, or being less than honest with friends. The first time a person crosses over the line into deceit is when they'll likely feel their intuition the strongest. But if they still decide to cross over into places they know they shouldn't, their intuition will quiet down most of the time. Intuition is not there to control you, it's there to guide you. So then it only pops back up –in full force – when a person is about to get caught, or nearly caught, in their behavior. If they're not caught, it quiets back down again after a short time. Something that also happens though is that the person develops an intuitive block because they know inside that they don't deserve what they have. In the case of cheating on a committed relationship, they always know inside that if the infidelity were found out, the person they're in the relationship with wouldn't be with them, and would definitely think less of them. If it's stealing from work, they know inside that any day could be the day they're found out and fired and/or charged with the crime. So what this does is give them insecurity because they don't feel good around the people anymore. Then instead of coming clean and choosing to be a better person, they subconsciously resent the person for "making them" feel that way. They'll try to tear the person down mentally or emotionally and show no empathy. This is because the shame they have inside is like a pit that sucks up all their emotions. They can't see outside of it, and can't see that they're hurting people who are being good to them and who trust them. To the people they are deceiving, especially after the infidelity or stealing are found out, it will be a shock and add massive injury to the injury they had already been experiencing.

If you are being honest and dealing with someone who is very dishonest, your intuition is trying to communicate with you as well. The important thing for you is to again pay attention to how YOU feel inside when around them or talking about them. Does your energy go up or down? Do you feel happy or distraught? Do you feel sure or confused? Most simply, do you feel good or bad? If a person in a relationship with you lashes out at you or becomes very critical, that doesn't feel good at all, right? Or if they don't celebrate your successes in life or worse yet belittle them or make them seem insignificant...that definitely doesn't feel good. You may believe the excuse that they haven't been in a relationship for awhile (how is that a valid reason for treating someone poorly?) or that they're having a difficult time with something in their life, or you may then believe that you are not worth as much as you thought, or that your accomplishments aren't as great as you thought they were if you listen to them. See, the tricky thing about this is that your intuition may be trying to tell you they're not being truthful, but you can only see what's in you. You are blind to what's not in you. If you are honest and trustworthy, it won't even occur to you that they may not be. That's why it's so important to keep the focus on how you are feeling and being treated. People who are in healthy relationships are supportive of each other and bring each other up. If a relationship isn't doing that for you, regardless of if they're cheating, if they've been lying to you about their own accomplishments, or if they've still got some other unresolved shame within them that they haven't dealt with and lash out at anyone who gets close or seems to have their life more together...you have to ask yourself why you're there if it doesn't feel good inside and brings you down far, far more than it ever elevates you. Maybe you'll find out the sordid details and it will make sense later and maybe not. But unless you'd like to take it on as an unpaid fulltime job which depletes your own emotional health and self-worth, you need to listen to your intuition and create distance when things feel awful inside around a certain person or group of people. Even if you really, really like them. It is your job and your responsibility to be honest and to resolve unhealed wounds within yourself. No one else can. It is not your job or responsibility to try to pull honesty out of someone or heal their unresolved wounds for them. You can't anyway, only they can. Instead of gratitude, you'll likely be scorned and told that you're controlling if you try. Don't go down that road. You can like a person, even love them, and decide based on how you're feeling and how you are being treated that they are not ready, willing, or able to be a healthy partner for you. Change doesn't happen overnight, so even if they profess their intention to change, staying close would put you in a "superior" position and them in an inferior which would again backfire because they would feel pressure and that they're not good enough, and you would need to keep lowering your standards and ignoring your intuition just to be able to be around them. This is one area that contains an enormous lesson; that which teaches you that trying to "help" someone be a better person is a great intention, but the method is very flawed. Losing yourself in trying to help someone find themselves will create in you an unfulfilled martyr and create in them more setbacks than gains in the long run because the only control they will feel is rebelling against what you're trying to do, regardless of if it's best for everyone or not. People have free will and they want to be able to use it. If it's not coming from within themselves, they're not doing it of their own free will. It's not the right time, and loving means letting go. Listen to your intuition. If something feels wrong, it probably is.

When a friendship, partnership, or relationship is honest and supportive, it feels that way. The connection lifts you when you're down, and increases your joys. You are honored and celebrated. Both silence and words are comfortable. The connection feels free. Everyone has baggage and emotional attachments and the closer you feel to someone, the more vulnerable you will feel. Now, if someone all of a sudden sounds just like one of your parents during a disagreement, it's up to you to decide and discern if you are projecting unhealed wounds onto the person of if they really are just like them. An open and loving partner can help you walk through the old rubble, and you can also help them. Those times don't always feel good, but it's because you are dealing with pain. That is part of emotional growth. It's important to be able to stay somewhat detached to be able to see when a great, open, loving relationship has its work and challenges, versus when a relationship is insecure and unstable and is almost nothing but a daily challenge. Journaling will help you to remain semi unbiased and detached, as you can go back and reread your thoughts from a week ago, a month ago, or more. You'll be able to see more clearly if you're experiencing a bad patch and working through it or if it's been that way for most of the entire relationship, just with different details. Keep your emotional focus and awareness on yourself. Allow yourself to move closer only to that which feels safe, free, accepting, trustworthy, and loving inside.

3 STRENGTHENING AND TRAINING YOUR INTUITION

Meditation is the best way to strengthen and train your intuition.

Meditation may sound like some fancy word and conjure up images of yoga pants or robe wearing people sitting cross-legged on a mountaintop, but it's really much easier than that.

Meditation most simply is just being quiet. Not quiet outside, but quiet inside. We have so many thoughts going on at all times. Many are perceptions of what is happening in the present moment but many, many more are reactions, triggers, memories, and links to things that are not in the present at all. What these do is most often completely take over the mind and totally remove you from the present moment. Meditation is a big, focused, intentional hush. Silence everything. Peace.

People often think that they need something to make them happy, or need something to stop or go away so that they can be happy, but in truth, "nothing" makes you happy. Wait, that didn't come out right... "the absence of needing anything to be different from what it is right now allows you to experience bliss, which is happiness." All those great things you want in the future; the upcoming vacation, the package from Amazon, the dinner date this Saturday, even the hour you'll get to relax after work...those are all things to look forward to and they are wonderful, but they do make the present moment seem less fulfilled than it really is because something "better" is coming in the future, or life might seem to be more fulfilled when that thing arrives or is achieved. The upcoming not-seemingly-good-things, the bill that's due, the court date, having to do the laundry...those on the mind when they're not occurring also can take away from the present moment because it may seem like life will be better once they are out of the way or done. And to the past, those great things that once were but aren't anymore, they can create a feeling of sadness that life isn't as good as it once was. Those not-so-good or even downright awful things that happened in the past, when remembered, they can trigger feelings of grief, sadness, anger, or regret if not forgiven, accepted or released because they hold a false sense of "if only." The false notion that "if only they hadn't happened the way they did, life would be better today than it is today." So good and not-so-good future and past can all be weights and barriers to being here, being happy, right in this moment. Meditation provides a space in which you can achieve bliss, because you'll train your mind to be fully present and suspend all thoughts, good and not-so-good, past and future. You will just be. Complete and fully aware only of the exact moment you are experiencing right at that moment. If you have achieved this before, you know exactly the freedom and peace contained here. If you haven't, oh you're in for a treat.

Something that comes up or can be a temptation is to then return to that state of bliss via meditation more than just part of the day. If it's so wonderful and so happy, what's the use of all of those other things that cause so much pain—emotional and mental pain especially? The use is that it's all part of life. Showers are great but you don't shower for five hours a day. Eating is great but doing it for ten hours a day wouldn't be so great at all. People differ, but meditation for most is best somewhere around 20 minutes to an hour a day, either once or once in the morning and once in the evening before bed. Aside from the checking in with awareness, being in a totally meditative state for hours and hours every day might seem like a super blissful thing to do, but eventually it would cause a disconnect between you and your world, between you and your relationships. You wouldn't be able to be as fully present with them and would become a little or a lot zoned out because of training your mind too much to be in that vast, slowed down, wide open space. To be in that frame of mind during meditation is amazing, but it's not the right frame of mind for most other times in life. It would probably end up being pretty frustrating for folks around you trying to keep your attention on their conversation while your mind drifts freely, contemplating the depths of reality and kind of ignoring their presence right in front of you. Just as your voice sound level adapts to the place you're in, be it church or a night club, your frame of mind and your chosen focus in different surroundings does best to adapt to what's best in that moment and be free to experience that moment with the frame of mind that is the most able to bring joy. So be a full on space cadet during your meditations but listen to and interact with your friends or family when they're having dinner with you and enjoy the sweet potatoes. Time and place. Don't lose interest in the small things or in the mundane or it will be difficult to enjoy anything outside of the meditative space. The everyday can be beautiful unless compared against the vast, meditative state. When compared, the everyday can develop a sense of apathy or pointlessness. That wasn't the point of meditation at all. You live here physically. Be here physically, and enjoy physical, tactile experiences. Especially the beach.

Your body requires in and out in the forms of exercise and rest, food and elimination, wakefulness and sleep. Your mind requires stimulation and relaxation, asking and receiving. Stimulation is accomplished in all daily activities. Whether you are in school or not, you are always actively learning. Relaxation can be deliberate or unintentional; it may be just sitting in front of a TV and not really paying attention but rather zoning out. Asking can be directly to others or in prayer. Receiving can be advice from a good friend or family member, or can be accomplished through meditation. If you don't meditate, and a lot of people don't, you may get caught up in or distracted by the opinions and needs of others and lose track of your own thoughts, feelings, and emotions along the way. You may have periods of "wake up" where you look back at the previous few months or years and think, "What was I thinking??" There's no peace in being a pinball on auto-pilot.

Here's a different water analogy...Imagine being out in the middle of the ocean. Not meditating is like being on the surface. Yes, you can see the sun, yes it's warm, and all around you are a million scattered waves, rising and falling in all directions. You bounce around on the waves, some smaller, some larger. This is where your surface emotions live; excitement, anger, and laughter. They are exciting for the moment and they come and go. They can be addictive because without them, things seem kind of boring.

But imagine for a moment that you can breathe underwater and the cold doesn't bother you at all. If you look below, it may seem dark and scary. But if you dive down, all the surface chatter ceases. It's a place that's feared by a lot of people because it's so quiet and still and all that noise is subdued.

But this is the home of your center of intuition.

This is the place where you can hear your own thoughts.

This is the ground from where your core emotions arise.

This is also the darkness that holds your past memories of trauma and joy. You know, both past trauma and past joy can hurt. Trauma, obviously because it was painful and thinking about it again relives the pain if you haven't made peace with it. But joy can also be very painful if it is a memory held tight of a person, pet, or time in your life that no longer exists.

A lot of new age work says "live in the moment," and that's true, but unresolved past feelings will unfortunately creep into the present moment and can ruin it if left unresolved. If you felt burned by love in the past and someone attempts to love you, those unresolved feelings will push away a beautiful new opportunity. If you still feel ashamed of some words or actions you said or took in the past, someone being good to you can also trigger the present moment action of pushing them away. This only happens when you haven't forgiven yourself and moved on.

You will always push away the things you feel you don't deserve, both good and bad.

If this only affected you, maybe it would be OK. It would be a place you chose for yourself and you should have the freedom to choose for yourself at all times. But in the case of love, it's not just hurting you. It's hurting someone else who did nothing wrong and doesn't deserve to be pushed away for being good and loving to you.

When you face your darkest moments and accept fully that they happened and let them go, let yourself go, you free yourself up and your entire future life to be a better person both to yourself and to others. In this deep, dark place you'll find peace. You'll also find your mind will quiet down and the chatter will cease. You'll become more decisive and know what's best for you and what you really want in life. If you don't know what you want, you may be subject to reacting from your ego instead of your soul. Chasing people and situations that reject you in order to try to feel validated, but then if they do accept you, the ego loses interest because the fight is gone.

In this quiet place, you'll learn that the fight is never really with another person or situation, it is always within yourself. You'll get to know your subconscious mind. You'll revisit past memories as the person you are now and see them in a different light. You will feel a great deal of release. Once you truly make peace with yourself, you'll lose the urge to fight with others or try to prove yourself to them and will seek peaceful interactions instead of adversarial ones.

You will find challenge in creativity and in improving yourself instead of in competition and in knocking anyone else down, or "winning" by having them lose.

You'll still win, but you'll be winning against yourself from the day before. You'll win by shedding old habits or thoughts that weakened you and will become a stronger, kinder, wiser person daily. You will lose your victim status and will become empowered. You will take responsibility for your life and your choices and lose the desire to blame others for making you or causing you to be stuck in bad situations or relationships that only cause you pain.

By accepting yourself, you'll accept others as they are now, too, and will be able to discern who you would like in your circle and who isn't compatible right now, letting go from a place of love instead of a place of anger. You will see the world much differently than you ever have before, and it will be beautiful.

Meditation keeps your awareness in the present and on those thoughts and feelings of yours. It keeps your mind clear and centered. It keeps the most important stuff at the forefront and improves your memory, mood, and decisiveness.

Aside from a specific 20 minutes to an hour, you can do awareness meditations many times a day for just a few minutes, including right when you wake up, in the shower, at a specific time each day, and right before you go to sleep.

Awareness meditations can be either intentional or centering. Intentional is for a specific reason or task and can also be called visualization or setting an intention. Centering, or "unintentional" is to get your mind in a quiet, grounded place and let any task or reason come to you. If you think of it like shopping, intentional meditation is like going to a certain store for a certain item or items and centering meditation is like just browsing around. Sometimes one is better than the other for different purposes.

A day may look like this:

1. Awaken:

Intentional meditation – Focus on self-confidence, happiness, decide it's going to be a good day. Everything you need to accomplish today will be accomplished in peace and on time.

Centering meditation – Relax the body, breathing in and imagining white light energy entering through the lungs and blooming throughout the body, charging it up with pure, beautiful energy that will last the day.

2. Shower/Morning Routine:

Intentional meditation – Think of the day ahead, possible interactions, things that need to be done, imagine yourself in those situations and accomplishing them with ease.

Centering meditation – Focus on each body part as you shower, keeping the mind free and putting your focus on the feeling and scent sensations; the water on your skin, the feel of the soap or washcloth on your skin, the scent of each product. Allow thoughts to enter your mind and observe them as they do.

3. Mid-day:

Intentional meditation – Checking in with your feelings, reflect on anything that took you out of your peace to this point, imagining the feelings float away even if something still needs to be resolved. Clearing and re-centering for the day.

Centering meditation – Taking a walk or sitting quietly and clearing the mind of any thoughts, giving your full attention to the present moment and then returning to the day.

4. End of work day:

Intentional meditation - Releasing any stressful or negative energy that collected and being able to be fully present at home or at plans for the evening. Choosing to be conscious and grateful of the time off with loved ones or alone.

Centering meditation – Listening to peaceful music on the drive home, releasing stress with each out-breath, shifting out of work mode and into home-life mode for the day.

5. Before bed:

Intentional meditation – Reflection of the day, focus on the good points and the good feelings, feeling grateful for them. Forgiving self and others for any bad points/bad energy even if things still need to be resolved. Letting go of the energy attached so that it doesn't stick. Thoughts of having a peaceful sleep and good dreams.

Centering meditation – Focus on the breath, while lying down, starting from the toes and working upwards, paying attention to any stress, muscle contractions in the feet, calves, knees, thighs, pelvis, torso, chest, arms, shoulders, neck, face, forehead, top of head and imagining any stress held there flowing out down through the bed, to the ground and being released with each exhale.

It may seem like a lot of work and while it's new and developing as an intentional habit, it sure is! It takes effort and diligence. But you do a lot of work every day to maintain the health of your physical body...showering, brushing, eating, drinking, cleaning, maintaining your surroundings, exercise...heck even tying your shoes seemed like a tough struggle when you first learned how, but now it's no work at all. Invest the time to develop the habits of awareness meditation. It will become a part of your routine after awhile and will be as essential to your mental and emotional well-being, nourishment, and hygiene as all of your physical actions are today. You'll wonder how you ever got along without it. Remember, too, that practice makes perfect. Don't give up if you forget a few times or if it stirs up some sensitive emotions and your first reaction is to shut them back down. Growing pains are a part of any growth.

A few of the benefits of active awareness are that your other senses improve. Well, they don't actually improve, you just become more aware of them so they become more noticeable and intense. Food tastes better, the fresh air smells better, clothing and sheets feel softer, and even the shower is more enjoyable. When you reconnect with your awareness and emotional and physical presence, you're not just locked into a mental loop existence of past and future, going through the motions and reacting. That mental loop can be somewhat of a dark cloud that dulls out everything else that's happening currently in your life. Once removed, the world feels better...from the tiniest details to the very big picture.

Benefits of Meditation:

Improved Memory: A lot of people think they have bad memory skills but really their minds are just overwhelmed with so many thousands of thoughts at once that nothing really sticks. It's all cluttered. A side benefit of meditation is that your memory will improve dramatically as your mind clears. It is a skill, and like any other skill that you've developed, it takes time and practice. But eventually you will become really good at it and it will become second nature.

Improved Sleep: A lot of insomnia is just the failure of the mind to shut down and let the body rest. By being aware of and in control of your mind and thoughts and learning how to direct the mind to slow down, you'll drift off to sleep much faster and be able to sleep through the night.

Stronger Intuition: For a lot of people who attempt to use their intuition, it's difficult to determine if what you're feeling is really intuition or just an unconscious link to something you've learned before. Particularly trauma...trauma is hard wired to become a reaction because in survival mode it may be the one thing that saves a person or not. So if you've survived trauma of any sort (especially childhood trauma) you'll be more susceptible to having what feels like strong negative intuition when it isn't that at all. It's buried fear.

Improved Health: Stress is a killer. Thoughts and events of daily life can really work a person up and cause all sorts of stress hormones to be released in the body. Higher blood pressure, adrenal overload and a weakened immune system are also common. Meditation lowers blood pressure, releases beneficial calming hormones, and brings the body back into balance. By making the time to meditate, you can literally improve your health today and your longevity for tomorrow.

Stronger Connection to Self: A great many people seek connection or what they call "love" through another person. But the most real and honest connection that you will ever have is with yourself. It transforms loneliness into solace, boredom into peace, and insecurity into confidence. Once you connect with your real self, you will begin to love and need to practice this place of peace on a daily basis or else feel a bit scattered. Getting there is almost like meeting a new person. You may have spent such a long time being so focused on doing, acting, saying, or trying to just be what everyone around you wanted that you lost much of the connection that you had to yourself naturally as a child. So to begin, the introduction will likely feel awkward, just like any other introduction. It may push some inner buttons or triggers like guilt or shame. But as you get to know yourself, you will find that you will much easier be able to forgive, let go, assert, and live without emotions flying off in any direction the wind happens to blow or in reaction to anything someone happens to say. It's not control like rigid or forced, but it's controlled emotions via being aware of your true feelings, the big picture, and the present moment, all within the space of the clarity that you develop within your own mind.

Types of Meditation:

Basic: The most basic type of meditation is either sitting cross-legged or lying down, eyes closed, focusing only on your breathing. Thoughts are scattered at first but eventually subside the more that you are able to focus on that in and out breath. The cool air coming in and the warm air going out. A slight pause in between the in breath and out breath, and becoming aware of the expansion and release of the air in the torso and the gentle rhythm of the heartbeat, relaxing all the muscles with each breath and tuning out the rest of the world. This is the most simple but also the most difficult to leap into. At first, it may take you five minutes of focus just to get one quiet second. For that reason, many other types of meditation can help guide you towards having the ability to get into this, the **meditative state** without any assistance at all.

Some of these other methods are:

1. **Spoken Guided Meditation:** An audio recording or live guided meditation where you listen intently to the speaker and are taken either just into a relaxed meditative state or along a journey to discover a specific aspect of yourself or your psyche. Similar to hypnosis, you will still be semi-conscious and aware of the speaker's voice but will enter a state of relaxation and focused awareness only to their voice and your present moment awareness of the place they guide you to.

2. **Tibetan Singing Bowls, Crystal, or Metal Singing Bowls:** If you've never heard singing bowls, it's not at all what you would expect it to be. A performer (or you) has a wand and runs it along the outer edge of a metal or crystal bowl which produces a clear, extended note and vibration at a certain frequency. Different sized bowls produce different frequencies. Some are purported to be specific to an energy center (chakras) and some are

designed just by the notes but claim to perform DNA repair or heal past lives. This may or may not be true, medical science is sparse on research. But sound healing has been practiced for thousands of years, even back to ancient Egypt, for medical purposes including blood diseases and tumors. For certain though, the singing bowls are much more effective in person than listening to a recording because of the vibration. In a recording, you only hear it, but live, you can feel it as well as hear it and the sound waves move through you. At group sessions with a performer playing the bowls, you will be lying down with eyes closed and able to just receive and open your mind. Many people experience great relaxation, visions, dream-like states, and are much more easily able to enter the meditative state. An Internet search will usually show you local yoga studios that hold singing bowl meditations. You can also purchase your own singing bowls online at thousands of stores and learn how to use them via YouTube Videos that demonstrate how to do it.

3. **Floating:** Floating is also called Sensory Deprivation and is done in a tank. The tank looks like a tear shaped clamshell hot tub but only has a few inches of water in it. The water is body temperature and is filled with hundreds of pounds of Epsom Salt (Magnesium Sulfate). You enter the floatation tank, close the lid, and float for an hour or more. You literally can't sink because of how much Epsom salt is in the water. You can relax every muscle, including your neck and just let go. Some people even float overnight. While in the tank, you basically shut out the entire world and all of its distractions. You are alone with your thoughts. All the pressures on the bones and joints release and you kind of lose track of where your body ends and where the water begins. People who float have a wide variety of different experiences, but most all are incredibly positive. Some people even say they communicate with aliens while floating. Who knows, maybe they do, or maybe it's just really deep levels of the imagination that otherwise aren't able to be heard. It's relaxing, it feels great mentally and physically to just let go of everything for awhile.

Also, the Epsom Salt bath makes your skin look vibrant and glowing and helps circulation of the blood. Wherever your mind goes; either just blank, into a dream-like state, or traveling the Universe is up to you. One thing about floating is that a lot of people are worried they'll feel trapped or claustrophobic in the tank. It's actually the opposite. Once you close the lid and lie back, you lose the awareness that you're in a small, closed pool and instead feel weightless and free.

4. Walking Meditation

Walking in a natural setting, the woods or on a beach, silently. Barefoot is better for a full connection. Listening to the sounds of nature, taking deep breaths, and focusing only on what surrounds you in each moment. Letting all other thoughts of the outside world, past and future, slip away.

4 RECOGNIZING INTUITIVE SIGNALS

Physically, you have neurons in your brain, stomach, and heart as far as we know today. Those neurons are the processing locations for things going on within those areas. They each may notice things before the other two catch on. In general, intuitive "no" is heavy, sinking, and tough to breathe deeply. Intuition "yes" is light, forward, expansive, pulling.

Your intuitive signals have been firing off your whole life, but most people haven't noticed them much at all. How is this possible? Have you ever needed a certain store and searched for it online and found that you drive past it almost every day but just never noticed it before? That's because you weren't looking for it. It was always there but it was not in your field of vision because you didn't think you had a need for it. Now that you are aware of it, you'll always know it's there. If you actually visited the store then each time you drive by, you'd also have conscious knowledge of what's inside the store…the people who work there, the layout, what they sell. It is the same as when you discover your intuitive cues. At first you'll wonder how you missed them. They've been there all along but you hadn't paid much attention to them before. Then, you may be a bit overwhelmed by the feelings you have constantly all day long. You will get accustomed to it as it develops into a new habit.

Things won't be clear right away but as you practice getting to know what the signals mean to you, what the feeling are, you'll get to literally know yourself better. You'll even be able to determine when you are receiving outside information or just a past trigger that you haven't quite worked through yet. Your world will truly transform from one that was unconsciously lived as mostly reactions to one that is lived in awareness from the inside out. Some folks call this detachment, but whatever you call it, it's a lot more peaceful.

How you feel around the people you choose to be around will give you a lot of insight into how you feel about yourself and about life.

Think about the people you see every day or every week. Think about the person you've chosen as your spouse, who your friends are, who your coworkers are, and especially if it's a big office, who you spend lunchtime with.

These people reflect your beliefs about yourself, people, life, and what you deserve, or what is real for *you*.

Now, you may think these people are all wonderful, really. But that doesn't mean that you feel *good* around them. Think of a person you think of very highly. Think of the last time or last few times you were around them.

Your biggest indicators of your beliefs are how you feel around two people,

1. The person you've chosen as a partner, whether that be serious boyfriend/girlfriend, husband/wife, or life partner, and

2. Your boss, closest coworker, or person you work with the most.

These two represent your dominant masculine and feminine influences. The first is a continuation of your mother and the second is a continuation of your father.

Even in a perfect childhood with wonderful parents, a child will have some negative feelings about themselves that they'll have to sort through and deal with in adulthood or they will keep repeating in an unhappy pattern. The mother figure or feminine energy represents the nurturer and the father figure or masculine energy represents the achiever. In households where the mother worked and the father raised the children at home, the masculine and feminine may be reversed from the genders.

When you consider how you feel around people, make a list of the five you spend the most time with. Although everyone can have good days and bad days, think overall about these, the Big Twenty:

1. Anxious or calm

2. Uncomfortable or comfortable

3. Inadequate or adequate

4. Less, more, or of equal intelligence

5. On edge or at ease

6. Judged or accepted

7. Disliked or liked

8. Unloved or loved

9. Unappreciated or appreciated

10. Unwelcome or welcome

11. Criticized or complimented

12. Angry or happy

13. Sad or joyful

14. Ignored or attentive to

15. Disregarded or valued

16. Not trusted or trusted

17. Unsafe or safe

18. Insecure or secure

19. Nervous or confident

20. Discouraged or encouraged

Become consciously aware of how you feel around people. It's important. Of course everyone wants to feel the latter of each of those feelings, but how you actually feel will tell you how you feel about yourself and what you believe is possible for you in this world. You're not attracted to stay around what you don't agree with, better or worse. If you feel you are not of value, you may at first feel good around those who do value you but you would soon question it and feel uncomfortable, even to the point of sabotaging the relationship or job so that you could seek the discomfort that you're used to elsewhere.

If you want to improve your relationships, it starts with you and your relationship with yourself. In order to identify that, you have to use the mirrors – the people and situations around you ⁓ to see the truth. When you do improve your beliefs about yourself, those around you may treat you better or they may leave, that part is up to them. But if they leave (or if you leave them), they will soon be replaced with people who reflect your current feelings about yourself and who you deserve to have in your life.

Basically, love yourself so that you can let other people love you, too.

The Big Twenty list can also be used to be able to identify which emotion you are experiencing. Each emotion has a different set of physical effects within your body. If you become aware of what exactly each one feels like to you, you'll be better able to discern them when they happen in the future.

For example if you look at #1, anxious or calm. Get yourself to a quiet place where you'll be able to be alone with this for 20 minutes or so. Sitting comfortably, close your eyes and take some deep breaths, focusing on the cool air coming in and the warm air going out, and the feeling of your heartbeat. After the scurrying thoughts of the day settle down, start with the first part: anxious. Think of a time when you felt really, really anxious. One may not come to you right away but sit still and think in your mind, "A time when I felt anxious." One should pop in. Relive that time, just for a bit to experience it. You may feel a weight in your stomach, or that your heart rate speeds up a little. You may feel your palms sweat, or a tension in your shoulders. Or you may feel something else entirely. This is how anxiety seats in your body. To keep track of this, write down what you felt in a journal. After you've identified everything that is anxiety to you, think to yourself, "I now release this past emotion and am free to return to today." Breathe in normally and push the breath out, as if to let that tension and feeling whoosh out of your body. Open your eyes and write down all you felt in your journal on the top half of a page marked "1. Anxiety."

If it's a bit overwhelming or you don't feel like doing any more, return to your day. If you'd like to do the other half (which feels much better!), go back into that meditative state, but this time, think, "A time when I felt calm." Again, breathe in and out with your eyes closed and allow the memory to float into your mind. This one should feel a whole lot lighter. You may even have a slight smile form on your face. You will probably feel a warmth in your heart area and a general feeling of bliss. Stay with this one for a bit and take note of how your body feels...are your shoulders relaxing? Do your arms feel lighter? Does your neck feel long? When you feel ready, open your eyes and again in your journal, write down how your body responded to being "calm." This second part can also be used as a meditation anytime you feel anxious about something that's happening in your life. Taking a break and rejuvenating your body is kind of like self-hypnosis. The event or circumstance that you need to deal with will still be there, but once you've moved your body into a more peaceful state, you'll be able to deal with it more effectively and with a much clearer mind.

Repeat these mini-meditations with the whole list of 20 and eventually you will have a journal that's become a guide book to your emotions. This is work, but with each one that you do, you'll get to know and master your emotions better. You can do it one a day until it's done, or take longer if bringing up those first emotions gets overwhelming. The second of each can be used as antidotes for the first whenever you experience them in life. You'll likely have more than one memory of each emotion pop up, and over the course of several meditations, some may reappear many times, or others that you haven't seen in years may make their way up to your conscious mind.

Whenever you return to the first ones, make sure to consciously release them before you come back to the present. Know that you are here and that memories from the past can be released to the past. They can't hurt you in the present. They don't exist anymore except as part of your life story. Letting them go won't leave you unprotected, it will free you to live more fully present and happy today.

5 TYPES OF INTUITION

There are many types of intuition. This by far is not a comprehensive list. Much of it can't be categorized accurately as it varies slightly and subtly from person to person. By doing the work of identifying and journaling what happens in your body with specific feelings from the last chapter, you'll be able to read yourself best and most accurately. The following may or may not be things you ever have, are, or will be experiencing along your journey.

1. Inner Weight Intuition

Earlier, in 'using intuition daily,' we discussed conscience. Conscience alone isn't all of intuition, but it is a part of it. Conscience is the mental processing of inner weight intuition. It activates when a lie is told, when someone is deceived, cheated, or even when the temptation to do any of those things arises.

Mentally, it is a general feeling of pressure and frustration. It's a discomfort that grows and is an inner weight and tightening in the heart and solar plexus area.

What this is, is a flare of the sense of intuition to correct the wrong, to set the course of the future right. Once truth is revealed, the weight is instantly lifted and there is an accompanying feeling of relief. The relief is felt even though the consequences of the truth coming out can be painful and/or result in the loss of significant relationships or status.

In the case of relationships where one is deceiving another, the one being lied to can also feel that pressure of the lie as the other is telling it to them. Intuition is from within, but it's not a closed system. Just as we can feel heat and magnetism, we can feel the intuitive energy of others when we are in close proximity. Speech is slowed, breaths are more difficult to take, and there's a feeling of hesitation and tension.

It's really important to become aware of and in tune with your conscience. Temptations happen. If you're bored or distracted in life, they may be more likely to happen than if you're focused and happy. But some decisions lead to paths that become really awful downhill spirals and aren't easy to step out of once they're entered into. Like jumping off a cliff, once you make that one, bad decision it can't be undone and large consequences follow. By recognizing your inner weight intuition, whether it's exactly like this or somewhat different, you could potentially save yourself from a whole lot of pain and snowballed choices that never had to occur because you became aware of and listened to your conscience the moment it fired and never stepped off that cliff in the first place.

2. *Wrong turn intuition*

Choosing a direction in life, whether it is relatively insignificant or life altering can bring about a myriad of thoughts, doubts, and feelings. What makes sense logically isn't always what feels right.

In the largest cases ~ the most important ~ wrong turn intuition can come into play. Have you ever been driving to a destination and realized suddenly that you've taken a wrong turn? Or turned down a street and realized it's a one way and you're going the opposite? These are varying degrees of wrong turns, and they cause the same feeling deep within as the wrong turn intuition when it comes to life decisions. It can be a mild quickening of the breath or it can be a deeply felt panicked feeling in the heart and upper chest area.

3. Inner Spark Intuition

Have you ever heard an idea or thought of something, or even saw an ad for some opportunity and felt just a little flicker in your heart area and perked up? That's a little inner spark. Something that you need to pursue. It may not be that first specific thing but something that appears when you investigate or direct more of your attention to that which ignited something within you. It may be an adventure awaiting, a business opportunity, or something that ends up changing your entire life. You'll remember that moment if you follow up on it as a seemingly insignificant but enormous moment in terms of awakening a part of you to something in a totally new direction. The seed that started it all.

4. Connection Intuition

Intuition about a person can be felt via connection. When meeting new people, people often glance quickly and shake hands but are paying more attention to remembering the person's name or aren't paying much attention at all. Even with this, people often feel a sense of if they have a good feeling about the person or a gut feeling that something isn't right. Just in that instant. Just in that split-second moment. It's so subtle that they can't pin it to any word, look, or action the person showed, but rather to a feeling they had inside. If there is something extra intriguing about a certain person that makes you both want to talk more or see one another again, you both have a lesson to learn from each other and a lesson to teach each other.

The brain may be clouding this type of intuition, so make sure to take time and use calm logic before thinking everyone you meet is your soul mate.

It could be that:

-the person looks like someone else you know
-the person sounds like someone else you know
-the person is in an unusually good or bad mood the first time you meet them, and you may be

picking up subconsciously on the energy *of that day*, but not their normal energy.

Again, that's why it's important to pay attention to your feelings but allow some more time to gather a few more feelings and process them before determining yay or nay. Even with scent, if you're not sure what a scent is, you keep on sniffin' it and put your attention to your mind to try to then process or figure out what it is, where you smelled it before, or what it smells like. With a few musical notes of a familiar tune, if you don't recognize it right away, even just hearing those few notes a few more times may pull up from your memory the rest of that song and the name of the song (along with where you were in life when you first listened to it).

5. Clairaudience

Clairaudience is hearing something within the mind that's not actually coming from a physical source. It's another way of processing intuition and happens more with people who have a really strong sense of intuition or those who have trained and been working with theirs for awhile. It may be a sound, like a bell or a whistle, or could be a thought voice that says a specific message. For example if you're talking to someone in person and they're telling you some grand tale about something they've made up and you're going along believing it until you hear within your mind, "yeah, right." Or it could be that you're about to go through a traffic light and you hear in your mind "STOP!" and when you do, a car whizzes through a red light and would have hit you.

6. Clairsentience

This is also more rare and specific, usually limited to real and claimed psychics. A lot of psychics who work with criminal investigators on missing person cases will use clairsentience. It operates under the belief that energy is stored within articles of clothing, homes, places, cars, things that people have touched or locations where people have been. By touching the objects of visiting the places, they feel experiences stored in the energy there. For them, "if these walls could talk" isn't a wish, but a truth. They see visions similar to flashes or premonitions but of things that have already happened, scenes from events that happened in those places or to people who have been there.

7. Clairvoyance

This is a term given to a very heightened sense of intuition, trained and skilled that perceives events or occurrences that are very specific and in the future. Famous clairvoyants are Nostradamus and Edgar Cayce. They may predict things that they see happening even hundreds of years after their deaths. Even Nicola Tesla had clairvoyant visions of the future. Rather than flashes or tiny snippets, a lot of clairvoyants have at length and very detailed visions, not much different than your most vivid dreams. It's as if they are living in that world briefly and are able to describe it in the same way as they would actually seeing it in real life and in current time.

6 INTUITIVE BLOCKS

Intuition is a feeling, a sense, but your brain is very closely tied to your own memory as well. Intuition will indicate a feeling now but that feeling may be affected by a mental or emotional wound or wounds from the past.

Have you ever had a cold and been totally unable to taste foods? When your nasal passages are blocked, your sense of smell just can't function properly. So if you were to taste the best apple pie in the entire world ever, you may shrug and say "meh, tastes sweet, not bad..."

If you have something blocking your energy, either temporarily (bad mood) or long term (past wounds), this can also happen with intuition. You may have someone or something right in front of you that is exactly what you've been wanting, hoping for, or believing in but be unable to recognize it because of your blocks.

Removing Blocks

This is kind of a catch-22 but more like your mind and heart working together in unison rather than one or the other or one always leading the other along.

If you have a "bad feeling" inside, that alone means only that there's a bad feeling. Meditating every day can help you to discover the root of that feeling – if it's likely internal or may be external.

Therapy and hypnotherapy in addition to meditation can help you to transition through intuition blocks as well as emotional limits or false beliefs. Therapy focuses on the logical, conscious mind. Hypnotherapy and meditation focus on the subconscious mind. The subconscious mind is your auto-pilot and was formed mostly when you were under the age of six years old. Things you may not remember at all could still be working against you and telling you that you can't be happy, that relationships always involve lots of arguing, or that money is only for other people but not you.

Triggers

Before having this awareness or undergoing any type of therapy or meditation, you may be unknowingly "overreacting" to certain things in life that others see but you do not. They just wonder why you overreacted. To you it was very real, but your subconscious holds the entire iceberg, not just the tip that was the cause of the overreaction today.

This is called "being triggered" because it only takes a little pull to cause a huge explosion, much like the pull of a trigger requires very little effort but results in a shotgun blast that does a lot of damage to whatever or whoever it hits.

For example if you were at work and someone said something that they didn't seem to notice but inside it was like you'd been hit in the solar plexus...had the wind knocked out of you. What WAS that?

The solar plexus is your self-esteem center, confidence, and action. It's in the center of your body, above your stomach and below your ribs.

When you meditate on that feeling, clear your mind and focus only on that area. Breathe deeply. You may have memories come up from your mental filing cabinet of other times you've had that feeling. Some of those times may be more obvious than others. The first one may not even be the hardest or most painful.

Solar plexus intuition is impacted when there is a perceived attack on your self-esteem, self-confidence, or an attempt to belittle you or make you feel small.

These may come in the form of

1. an insult

2. being told you can't do something

3. laughing, mocking, teasing, which are all disempowering actions

So maybe the root of this was way back on the playground being bullied. Maybe it was in a relationship that started out great but ended very badly. It could have been being told by a parent or an authority figure that you'd never amount to anything in life. Or, maybe it was in being told you could do something and then having that promise broken. Some kind of a rejection, or even a feeling of being trapped that made you feel small and powerless.

This is also a trigger point for the fight, flight, or freeze response. This is because it's an action center.

Have you noticed that a lot of people "snap" when they feel they are rejected or trapped? This isn't a coincidence. This is a shutting off of the logical brain and going into emergency survival mode of attack or flee for life. They have just been triggered and their pain fired outward.

Triggers are deeply tied to past pain. They are an

insurmountable block to happiness and healthy relationships *if* they are allowed to remain. The survival centers of the brain override the non-survival centers because when they are needed, it is literally life or death. Since the body's main objective is to keep the body alive, this only makes sense. But just as sometimes people have an overly reactive allergic (anaphylactic) response to peanuts or bee stings, it's not the peanut or bee sting that can kill people, it's the body's over reaction. The way to cure a trigger is to identify it and then heal it. If it is not cured, it will keep showing up where it doesn't really exist, and will harm every close relationship you ever have.

We've all experienced deep pain. We all have triggers. Many people unknowingly choose to not heal and instead blame the world for their anger and insist that it's real. They hurt people who have done nothing wrong but they don't feel any remorse because in their reality, they are the ones being hurt.

The Energy and Beliefs of Those Closest To You

While it is true that no one can "make you" feel or think any certain way, those closest to you do influence you and your energy does mix with theirs. Jim Rohn said that "you are the product of the five people you hang around the most." So if you're trying to open up your mind and make better use of your intuition, those people who surround you may not want to also jump on board. Talking with them about your experiences is great, as long as they are positive and supportive and open minded, too. If not, you may find that they believe their reality is wiser or somehow more realistic than one that includes the use of Intuition, and you may find that telling them about your experiences isn't fun and sometimes even turns into an argument. You don't have to talk them into anything. Just do what you do and enjoy it. If you have a friend who already uses their Intuition and loves to share stories with you, that's great! Adding passionate, joyful energy to the experiences will cause them to expand in a positive way. You may even go to local meditation groups alone or together to connect with others who are more interested in using it, too. A lot of yoga studios have some kind of meditation within their yoga classes or as separate events or classes outside of the yoga class times. You don't have to get rid of anyone who disagrees with you. That would be a mistake. Just realize if it's not a topic that you agree on and can discuss positively – like politics! – and especially while you're new at it, avoid talking about it with people who think it's silly or have no interest. You can make better use of your energy elsewhere.

Clearing the Mind Clutter

Mind clutter consists of all those thoughts that repeat and flurry about in your mind throughout the day. Most of them are necessary, but not now and not repeated so many times. Things you have to do, appointments, things you're running low on in the fridge, people you need to call, bills you need to pay. All these things can be managed much more easily via lists and calendars. Get a big old wall calendar and post it in the kitchen. Write on it any future day plans or appointments that are more than a week away. Before making new plans, check the calendar. Every night before bed, check what's coming up the next day. That way, you don't have to keep thinking of what's coming up or worry about making plans to do two things at the same time. Lists for groceries of course on the fridge are helpful because the grocery store is distracting with all that's on sale and all that's new. When you're in your home, you're conscious of what you need to replenish. That is the place that will be easiest to make the list, adding to it as it develops instead of sitting down and trying to write a whole one up at work, being totally out of the home environment. Your mind can be very focused on the place you're in right now, and as you train it to become more aware of the present moment and space, you might seem to become more forgetful, but really you're in your current time and space fully. You may find that without lists, you think you got everything at the store, but on the way home remember a few things that you wonder how you could have forgotten. This is because your mind on the way home is transitioning between the store and the home and refocusing on your life in that space. A list on your desk of "to-do" and keeping all incoming bills kept with that list in due date order can help to free up the mind from worry about things not getting done that have penalties if they're not done by a certain time. Or auto-pay for bills is another option to achieve the same. The calendar, grocery list, and to-do list are such easy habits to pick up and develop that they may seem insignificant but they free up so much space on your mind's internal memory hard drive. When you try to keep all these thoughts in the forefront of your mind at all times in an attempt to not forget anything, they end up in a big pile, filling your mind and repeating, taking up far more space than you realize. If you imagine your mind as a large table, and each thought as a sheet of paper, imagine the stacks you'd have if each repetition created another sheet of paper every time. Your desk would soon become loaded up and you'd be more likely to miss the exact thought needed at the exact time because of the disarray. A clean table with three drawers (date calendar, grocery list, to-do) and placing each thought in one of those drawers and going to that exact drawer only when necessary would leave your table clean and able to focus on what is placed upon it now, or to fulfill the contents of each drawer at the right time.

7 FLASHES, PREMONITIONS, DREAMS, AND PSYCHICS

Psychics; are they real? Some people have an incredibly strong sense of intuition. They may have noticed it early in life and if it was developed or encouraged by their parents, they could very well have a much better developed sense than many other people. Also training or psychic school is more common than you may realize. It's not witchcraft but rather ways to tap into or recognize more and more about the sense and how to use it effectively.

Just because they pick up something and tell you about it, it doesn't mean you need to check in with them daily or even do what they say. There are people who have fantastic senses of smell and taste who can tell if there is one grain of black pepper in a dish. They can discern and determine a great deal about a bowl of soup that you cannot. But...they can't tell if you'll like it or not. They can only tell if they will. It's still up to you to decide what you will or won't do. A good real psychic won't tell you what to do. They may only describe things that have happened or possible outcomes and that's not really far off from a psychologist. A psychologist can tell usually by what a person believes if they've had any certain type of trauma based on how human beings act and react in general to those types of traumas. We're very complicated in details but very simple in basics. So to see a general psychic or to see a general psychologist or even counselor, priest, rabbi...use it more for unbiased advice into your own psyche from a source that you trust. People who don't believe in psychics will never be able to be helped by one because their energy is completely unreceptive to the knowledge that psychic has to offer. But if they heard identical advice from someone they believe is a source of wisdom, they may be ever grateful to have heard it.

Be open to be able to receive information that could be helpful, but use your own discernment and judgment as to what to do with your own life because you know your truth better than any other person in the world ever has or ever will.

Flashes:

A flash is a split second image, thought, feeling, or knowledge of something that you couldn't possibly know from any other source. It may be current time, past revelation, or future premonition.

Current time flashes happen most often connected to a loved one; you know the second someone you love was in an accident or in trouble. It stops you cold in your tracks and comes with a sense of urgency. You may see an image or just have such a strong feeling that you cannot ignore it and must call the person immediately. Current time flashes may also be a call to immediate action for your safety. Some people who have avoided accidents have heard a voice in their mind say, "stop!" or "turn left!" so clearly that they did so and then saw a car run a red light or spin out of control right where they would have been.

Past revelations are usually in images, a split second moment from a time past. What's happening currently may not have any relevance to the past revelation, but it, for that brief second, appears as clear as if it were happening in front of you. It may be something you'd totally forgotten about or something you remembered but not recently. When a past revelation occurs, it's an "a-ha" moment of clarity on something in your life that was as of yet unresolved.

Future Premonition flashes also seem to appear out of nowhere but they are usually connected to a loved one or close friend who you may be speaking to at the moment they happen. It comes as a quick thought or an image in your mind and it's so strong that you may feel the need to ask them about it right then and there, even if you had been in mid-conversation before that moment about something totally unrelated. If you are a very empathic person and a friend is asking about a problem or concern they have, this future premonition flash may be an acknowledgement that they are on the right path or something that seems to discourage their current path.

Flashes, for those who don't know about them, are usually jarring and unsettling. They are perfectly normal, however, and will increase for people who take time daily to meditate and clear their mind. They are always helpful but not overly intrusive or controlling in nature. You or the person they are about are still in full control of your own choices and destinies. Flashes are just a flicker of illumination along the way.

Premonitions

Premonitions aside from flashes may be much longer and may come in the form of dreams or even daydreams. They often serve as a warning of a future event and series of events that lead up to it. They can be centered around a certain relationship and are mostly feelings based; definite, uneasy, suffocating, and even an impending doom feeling as long as the path or relationship continues. If the path is consciously changed, the feeling can "break" as if coming out from under water. A feeling of relief and freedom occurs and strengthens as time goes by and that destructive path dissolves further and further into impossibility.

Dreams

Dreams for the most part do not contain future premonitions but rather emotions and feelings regarding present circumstances and how the past led up to them. Recent and long ago past experiences all affect life today. Dream symbols, especially in particularly vivid dreams, can tell you things about your emotions and actions that you otherwise may not be aware of in daily life. When you remove the conscious world, the subconscious has time and space to speak directly to you. There are lots of websites that interpret dream symbols. One excellent one is www.Dreammoods.com . It has a searchable database and the interpretations are strange at times but often very accurate.

To understand your subconscious better, keep a daily record of your dreams with a little notepad or recorder beside your bed. As soon as you wake up, jot down or speak notes on what was in the dream ~ and most importantly~ how you felt during circumstances that were going on in the dream. For example, in the dream you may have been speaking to a person. Who that person was plays a factor, but how you felt towards that person in the dream matters more. Usually the person isn't that person but an aspect of yourself or of how you view life reflected back to you. If a person is famous or in a position of high authority, it may be your subconscious speaking to you about your own abilities or limitations, or how you view attention or authority. If the person is someone you know today or knew long ago, think of one or two words you would use to describe that person...the dream is more about those qualities in you and how they play a role in your life and relationships.

8 TELEPATHY, MIND-READING, AND INFLUENCE OVER OTHERS

The more you meditate, the quieter your mind becomes. The quieter your mind becomes, the more open it will be. The more open it is, the more you will be able to see, hear, or feel those energies around you that are subtle whispers that used to be drowned out by all the mind chatter that was going on in your mind before. Even if you're not deliberately trying to read someone's mind or become telepathic, it will happen from time to time.

Now, the more you know someone, the more aware you are of their moods and body language. So to people you know, you may not notice any difference at all. And if you're a bit guarded around strangers, as most people are, you may not pick up on any thoughts, feelings, or energy coming from them.

Psychics who are in the business of being psychics (not fake ones) are open to the thoughts and energy of strangers because they are intentionally open to them. Just like anything else, the more a person practices, the stronger their abilities become.

For most people, it's really not advisable to become so focused on what other people are thinking or feeling because it takes your attention away from your own awareness and your own feelings. If a person's intentions towards you are bad, you don't have to pay attention to them or figure out exactly what they are in order to protect yourself. If you're paying attention to your own feelings, those will tell you much louder and more clearly that something isn't right. Ultimately, your intuition is for you, for your life, and to guide you through it. Respect other people and their own free will and recognize that they, too, have been given intuition and can choose to use it or not to guide their lives. You may have ideas, thoughts, or whole plans in your mind for how they should live their life and decisions they should make and you may be 100% right. But....just as you want to be in control of your own life, loving them and respecting them means allowing them to be in control of their own life, too...even if they trust your opinion, even if they believe in your intuition more than their own. The best you can do for them is to encourage them to get quiet and discover and develop their own inner voice and listen to it. They may even come to the same decisions and choices that you thought were best for them, but if they don't, it's not your place to correct their path. We all learn at different paces. Confidence and discernment are only developed by making one's own decisions using their own free will and with no outer pressure. This can be really difficult with adult children, but ultimately, remember that it's not your job to drive their life. It was your job to prepare them to drive their own. Once they became adults, your advice once in awhile can be helpful, but if they're seeking your advice over their life decisions, you'll take credit or blame for the results and they won't know what to do when the time comes that you're not around. Be a soft place to fall and encourage them to get back up again when they make what turns out to be a wrong decision, but don't try to talk them out of or pre-empt them from making those adult choices that will determine the course of their lives. Even though it may seem like helping in the short term, it's damaging in the long term and there's no going back.

You can like a person but still get a bad feeling about them. When you like them, you tend to project innocent reasons for the bad feelings. For example if you get a bad feeling around a potential romantic interest, you may excuse their reactions, behavior or energy by thinking "they must have been hurt before," or "they're not used to being in a relationship and they are afraid of commitment or nervous." While this may be true, it's best not to automatically assume the best about everyone all the time. Give the benefit of the doubt and be open, but also be aware and observe as unbiased as you can when you see red flags pop up. Otherwise, you'll regret not paying attention later on down the road if it turns out they had manipulative or deceptive intentions and you knew something was off right from the start.

Also for the most part, telepathy can be fun. It has happened to almost everyone at least once where they've thought of a person seemingly at random and then the person messages or calls them soon after.

Being interested in telepathy with other willing participants is one thing, but relying on it over actual real, live communication is not a good idea. The connections you form in your brain become stronger the more that you use them. There are people who started out thinking they picked up a thought or two from someone and then became so focused on it that they honestly believe they hear full conversations from people when really it's entirely their imagination. On the very dark side, this is what can happen with people who stalk celebrities. They believe they have been communicating telepathically with the celebrity for days, weeks, or months, and no one can tell them any different because it seems so real to them.

The brain is a very complex system and reality truly does depend on perception.

So most simply, don't even go there. It's far better to use your actual intuition just for your own wellbeing and keep communication between yourself and others to in-person conversations, texts, emails and phone calls. That way you can be sure you'll never tread into territory that is completely make-believe.

9 THAT'S SOMETHING, BUT IT'S NOT INTUITION

From the inside, some people are convinced their intuition is telling them to do things. Something is telling them to do things, but it's not intuition. Maybe you'll never need this chapter. Hopefully, you'll never need this chapter, but in case you ever do, or if you're ever confronted with someone who believes these things, please remember it.

1. Pursuit of "Love" that isn't Love

People who stalk others sometimes believe that their intuition or God is telling them that this person is "the one," and no matter what the person tells them or how many restraining orders they receive, they don't listen to outer reality because they are convinced that their inner voice should be trusted over all else. Unfortunately, a lot of generic quotes or social media posts may even seem to support this type of thinking. Yes, listen to your gut. Yes, listen to your heart, but also, be aware of what intuition isn't, and if there's a voice inside your head telling you to pursue someone who just isn't interested, know that's not your intuition. It's something, and definitely seek out a qualified health professional such as a psychologist or therapist (not a psychic who encourages you to follow it) to get to the bottom of what it is, but don't follow it.

Intuition comes from your higher self. This higher self is infinite wisdom and love. This means respecting the spoken wishes of others and detachment from what you may think you want. Really, why would you want a person who isn't interested in you? Why not let them go and send them love and wishes of happiness to find someone who they are interested in? You need to love yourself and accept who you are today. That's not to say you'll never improve yourself, but only change and improve yourself for you...not to try to become what you think someone else wants. If you change to try to become what you think someone else wants, they may change their mind when you've done so, and you'll always be after a shifting goal. Focus on you. Become your best self. Allow those who don't appreciate you to move on out of your life. You have nothing to prove to them and winning them over by losing yourself is not a worthwhile goal.

2. Harming Others

A lot of awful things happen when people think they are listening to their intuition, God, Allah, or whomever they believe is the voice inside their head. Your intuition will never, ever, ever instruct you to harm another person. Thoughts about envy, revenge, or outright hatred have to be dealt with and dissolved, not pursued. Pursuing those thoughts and feelings will only make them stronger and stronger until they turn from thoughts to words and then actions. Whatever that voice is inside your head telling you to do that, it's not right and it's definitely not God. Don't listen to it. Seek out help to silence it if you're not able to do it on your own. There have been many attacks and murders done because angry thoughts turned into blind rage and all it ever brings is pain and destruction. Not justice, not settling any scores, and definitely not redemption of any sort. People run with thoughts of revenge because it makes them feel temporarily empowered when they have felt hurt and powerless. In a dark fantasy they become the hero or heroine over their pain by striking down those who they feel were responsible, but the truth is that if they act on it, they only become one of many victims. For the person committing the act, aside from the voice in their head, their entire body is trying to tell them not to do it. But because they feel that surge of excitement and/or believe it is the will of their higher power or a warped sense of justice, they ignore everything else and do so much irreparable damage to so many people. If you hear someone you know expressing hateful or threatening words towards a person or people, distance yourself for safety, but report their words to the police. Thoughts turned into words and threats have already gained enough momentum to do so. If they are having these thoughts, they are suffering, too. Laws in many places allow for mental health evaluation and treatment based on threats to harm others, but no doctor can do anything if no one says a word. Some people give no indication of awful things they plan on doing and those unfortunately can't really be avoided except by the person themselves. But a lot of people do begin to act strangely and give off clues that something is happening to their mind that they are not in control of. Telling on them is the kindest, most courageous thing you can do to help them and others who they may end up harming in the future.

3. *Childhood Programming*

When you were a child, what you learned about life and love became your truth. As you grew up, those beliefs took root in your subconscious mind. When you meet people who seem familiar, it may be that they resemble your primary caregivers; your mother and father or whoever raised you. This is fine and good if all was well. But if you had an abusive or traumatic childhood, you may be drawn to people who exhibit the warning signs of being abusive for the very fact that they are familiar to you. You may likely find yourself in a relationship that closely resembles that of the one your mother was in with your father or vice versa. This reliving of the past is a pattern that most people unknowingly recreate even if they really, really don't want to. You can't really go by signs or signals to identify people to avoid, but you can work on yourself so that you'll not be attracted to those types anymore no matter what signs they give off. Working on yourself through self-help, therapy, hypnotherapy, meditation, and the basic loving and accepting yourself will help to rewrite your childhood programming and free you from the chains and pain of the past. You may only discover some things within the recreation of those relationships. Your intuition, no matter how highly developed, will not steer you away from certain life lessons that have to be lived and experienced in order to be learned. Within those situations, if you are aware of your intuition, it will help guide you through in the best way possible. Your inner child took the blame for pretty much anything that was wrong because children believe adults are all-knowing, perfect people so anything wrong must be your fault. To unlearn those core beliefs in adulthood takes time. Even in perfectly wonderful childhoods, children will perceive things that aren't true. For example, a child may believe a parent's work is more important than them if the parent has to work a lot just to pay the bills. The child may develop a disdain for work because it's associated with pain, for money for the same reason, or believe their time isn't valuable because no one made time for them. None of those things are or were actually true, but were very true in the child's perception at the time.

PTSD, childhood trauma, and trauma from really damaging relationships or life events can cause people to become overwhelmingly possessed by fears, sadness, anger, or all of these things. Those feelings and beliefs are dangerous and can dominate every thought, leaving no room for peace, love, and actual intuition. They will instead be guided by paranoia, revenge, hatred, greed, and push away or destroy good things and people and cause a lot of pain to themselves and others. Mental and emotional pain as well as often turning physical to violence. I believe in evil acts, not evil people. Evil acts are carried out by people who are either trapped in pits of despair and see no other way out or who are terribly misguided in what they believe is the "right" thing.

When you are dreaming, you could be on a battle field being chased by a giant whale who is shooting at you with a donut gun. As ridiculous as it would be after you woke up, while sleeping you would believe every second of it because in your dream belief system, anything is possible. There are no limits to "reality." So just trying to logically talk someone out of their PTSD influenced reality won't work...to them it IS real and IS terrifying and they do need help to be able to wake up from that nightmare. Calling the police on them isn't "telling on them" or "getting them in trouble." It's helping them, or at least trying to.

10 CHAKRAS

There are 7 main energy centers in the body along the spine from root (tailbone/base of the spine) to crown (top center of head). Each energy center represents an intuitive feeling and will be activated accordingly. Sometimes more than one is activated. Physically, they are connected to glands and are responsible for triggering many biochemical reactions either within the gland, or signaling the brain from those centers.

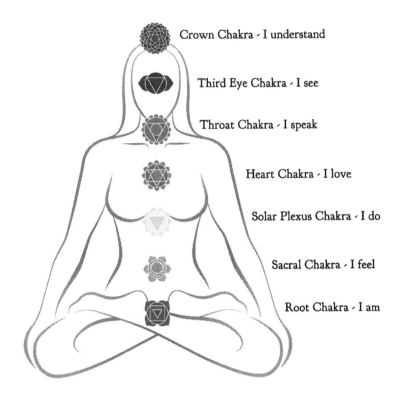

Crown Chakra - I understand

Third Eye Chakra - I see

Throat Chakra - I speak

Heart Chakra - I love

Solar Plexus Chakra - I do

Sacral Chakra - I feel

Root Chakra - I am

There is so much information on Chakras, you could probably find a million books and that many videos and articles online. This is just a very basic overview just of the physical signals from each of the chakras as they relate to intuition and emotions for those who haven't really heard of them before, or a refresher for those who have.

1. Root Chakra: Survival and Physical World.

Color: Red.

Location: Base of the spine.

When threatened, the effect can be as traumatic as emptying of the bowels. Can also feel like a lightning strike up the spine, originating at the base. Other low, weakened, or blocked energy signs are clenching, tightening, constipation, diarrhea, or general discomfort.

Open and flowing energy in this center is associated with bowel regularity, stamina, and physical energy. Strengthen this chakra with walking and good, nutritious foods.

Statement: I am.

2. Sacral Chakra: Creativity and Relationships.

Color: Orange.

Location: Sacral area of the spine/sex organs

A blocked, low energy, or weakened sacral chakra in women can lead to painful menstruation/cramps/PMS. Worse than normal. Impotence in men, lower back pain, or loss of sex drive.

Strengthen this chakra by spending time alone in creative pursuits, and fostering good, loving relationships by being loving, honest, and trusting as well as trustworthy. Create boundaries and standards for healthy relationships. Release feelings of shame and guilt and stop doing any of the things that cause those feelings, like lying, cheating, or deceit.

Statement: I feel.

3. Solar Plexus Chakra: Self-esteem, confidence, action.

Color: Yellow.

Location: Solar Plexus (above the navel, below the sternum)

When threatened, it feels like you've had the wind knocked out of you. A blocked, low energy, or weakened solar plexus chakra energy feels like shrinking, curling around the solar plexus, rounded shoulders, or middle back pain.

When open and flowing, it feels like you are very empowered to do something, with bold confidence in the action. Positive expectation and excitement. Strengthen it with positive, confidence building statements and by trying, doing, and achieving things you want to do instead of just thinking about doing them or procrastinating.

Statement: I do.

4. Heart Chakra: Unconditional Love for self and others.

Color: Green or Pink.

Location: in the heart area.

When threatened, it feels like a sudden sharp stabbing pain in the heart. Low energy, weakened, or blocked feels like a heavy, clouded feeling. Draws even the face downward in sadness. Disconnection.

When open and flowing, it feels light and open. Strengthen this chakra with acknowledgement of self-worth, accept and unconditionally love yourself fully, have joyful experiences, and a whole lot of appreciation and gratitude. You can have unconditional love for everyone and be safe. Unconditional love is only how you feel about them, whether they are in your life or not. Conditional presence in your life is a healthy boundary to protect you if anyone is not ready, willing, or able to treat you with kindness and love, too.

Statement: I love.

5. Throat Chakra: The voice. This is the connection between what the heart feels and what is expressed to the world. It is the pathway to truth.

Color: Blue.

Location: the front of the throat.

When the throat chakra is blocked, low energy, or weakened, the voice cracks, the person may feel the need to cough or clear their throat, or they lose their voice altogether. This can happen suddenly during a lie, the throat closes up or the voice comes out in a very high pitch.

When open and flowing, the voice is strong and clear. Relief after difficult words are spoken. To strengthen this chakra, sing or hum, and speak your truth, always. You don't have to give every detail to everyone. To those closest to you, things that affect their life should not be secrets. To acquaintances or strangers asking about your personal business, the truth can be "I don't feel comfortable sharing that with you," or, "thank you for asking, but that's personal."

Statement: I speak.

6. Third Eye Chakra: This is the major intuition center also called the third eye.

Color: Purple.

Location: in the center of the forehead just above the eyebrows.

When blocked, low or weak energy, the person may experience headaches, blurred vision, anger, wrinkled or furrowed brow, and frustration.

When open and flowing, there's an understanding of another person and their point of view with no need to argue or prove one's self as "right." To strengthen this chakra, understand that right and wrong for the most part are only a matter of perception. Make peace of mind a goal and practice deciding if something is worth giving up that goal for the moment or the day, or not. Accept of what is versus what you think should be. Practice the Serenity Prayer. Let go and move on from things that are not right for you. Realize that your time is valuable and spend it well.

Statement: I see.

7. Crown Chakra: Seeing the bigger picture. Connection to the highest self and or, God, Allah, Spirit, or whomever one's religion believes is the overseer of the Universe.

Color: White.

Location: the top center of the head.

When low, weak, or blocked energy, there's a feeling of being isolated, stuck, limited, or depressed. Caught in current struggles.

When open and flowing, there's an inner knowing that trials have a reason. To strengthen this chakra, face your challenges, practice empathy and seeing outside of yourself and your own circumstances.

Listen to "the other side" before making a judgment. Believe in the good in people. Rise above pettiness and drama and see the bigger picture.

Statement: I understand.

Traditional heterosexual roles of men and women have had men primarily dominant in the lower three chakras, women in the upper three, with them connecting in the middle at the heart.

The lower chakras are more concerned with the physical and material world; the physical body, sex, action over thinking about things, building, and inventing –creative methods and products.

The upper chakras are more of the inner world; thoughts, emotions, compassion, intuition, and communication.

Everyone has the ability to develop and strengthen all of their Chakras. Developing strength and freedom in all chakras doesn't make a man into any less of a man and doesn't make a woman into any less of a woman. They make each person more developed, mature, and independent as a whole and less reliant on someone to parent their underdeveloped needs. Choosing to be with someone as a partner instead of being fearful of needing them for survival. In homosexual relationships, masculine and feminine energies are usually stronger in one person and weaker in the other. This creates the attraction and a balance between the union.

In heterosexual couples, the energies can also be partly or fully reversed from the traditional roles as well. Regardless, each person can develop all energies and transform relationships from fear based need to love based choice and become more confident in themselves and free to love fully without attachment. To be with someone because you want to be, not because you think you have to be.

Kundalini Yoga in particular focuses on Chakra energy, opening the chakras and releasing blocks to energy via specific motions, mantras, and meditations.

Tibetan Singing Bowls, mentioned earlier, also are supposed to assist in cleansing and opening chakras based on the sound frequencies they emit which are matched to each chakra.

Walking barefoot in the grass or at the beach is supposed to be great for "grounding" the energy of all the chakras. Some people call it "earthing." Clearing out any static type energy from the body and discharging it into the ground. Through the hands, this can be accomplished through gardening. Basically a connection between your bare skin and the Earth. There have actually been scientific studies that showed the interaction between the Earth's electrons and our bodies has health benefits including better sleep, reduced stress, and pain reduction.
Source:
https://www.ncbi.nlm.nih.gov/pmc/articles/PMC3 265077/
The theory is that we used to sleep on the ground and walk barefoot and were much more in contact directly to the Earth for many hours a day than we are now with pavement and living indoors and

synthetic soled shoes. Weather permitting, it may be a good idea to take your shoes off and go stand in the yard and reconnect, even if only for a few minutes (and at risk of odd stares from the neighbors). Or of course go to the beach and get those toes in the sand.

Whether you "believe in" chakras or not, you can still use the information psychologically to focus on and develop your thinking in a positive and empowering way. By focusing on each of the chakra statements, you can create powerful affirmations and also use them in meditations to get to know your feelings, limitations, and beliefs.

For example, the root chakra statement is "I am." Write a list of some "I am…" statements about who you are or who you wish to be at your best. For example, "I am courageous." If you go into the meditative state and think only this statement repeatedly with pauses in between, you will begin to scan your mind and memory banks for proof of the truth of this statement as well as proof that it isn't true. Take comfortably deep breaths and take your time. Which memories come to mind? Feel gratitude to your younger self in situations that you are reminded of where you were very courageous. The ones where you were not, forgive yourself. Realize that unpreparedness, fear, and panic can lead people to instinctively make one of three choices; fight, flight, or freeze. So maybe in a couple of situations you avoided them or were more meek than you'd like to have been because you were afraid of who was on the other end of your courage. Accept that things happened the way they did. Let go of any resentment you hold towards yourself and decide that even though you may not have acted courageously in those instances, it doesn't mean that you're not a courageous person.

You are a courageous person and if something similar presents itself in the future, you will handle it differently. You will handle it with love and courage. Embed that into your subconscious and the next time something like that happens again, your courageous instinct will take over. That doesn't mean you'll start getting into fights, it just means that you'll be able to respond from a strong mental place instead of reacting from a fearful one.

Another example taking the sacral chakra statement, "I feel" could be, "I feel valued." This one probably will have a lot of baggage come up from when you were very young while you're in the meditative state. You'll revisit times when the child in you felt not very valuable, but you'll be able to see them from an adult point of view.

Remember, children believe that adults know everything and so when things go wrong, they blame themselves. If the parents argue, it must be their fault. If the parents complain about money, it must mean they are to blame for costing too much. It isn't true, but if you don't revisit these memories and clear them out as an adult, the only thing that's there is the old childhood memory that's been carried all these years.

This one and others like it dealing with self worth and love can bring up some overwhelming emotions of sadness or even anger. They may be better handled with a therapist or hypnotherapist guiding you through if you're having trouble doing it alone. It's important that you purge them, and having difficulty doing it doesn't mean you're weak at all. It probably means you have a great capability for love and empathy and the amount of courage it takes to face and purge them is enormous. Freeing yourself from subconscious feelings of not being of value will improve your life, your sense of self, your confidence, and your relationships. Feeling of little or no value causes people to put themselves in places and relationships where others treat them that way. It's a match to the subconscious belief. Raising the belief of value will raise the outer mirrors. Not by magic or woo woo manifestation, but because you just won't accept or be attracted to places or people who treat you so poorly. You'll be able to walk away without any desire to prove your value to people who don't see it. That desire comes from the unhealed inner child. Once healed, he or she is free to move along to better, brighter pastures with no need to prove their value to anyone.

Keep in mind that the years of your experiences and knowledge were applied moment by moment, day by day in layers that can't be unraveled and undone in one fell swoop. Plus you've got moments now and layers forming as each day goes by. Becoming aware of your feelings, emotions, reactions, and checking in with your mind and feelings for 20 minutes a day in meditation will help to identify those patterns that have been repeating and change their direction if they've proven to lead to poor results in your life.

Some changes in life will be abrupt, others will be way more subtle, but all will become more true to you ⸺to your best self⸺ as you get to know and love you better.

ABOUT THE AUTHOR

Doe Zantamata was born and raised in Canada near Toronto. She attended university at Niagara University for two years before transferring to Florida State University and holds a BSc. in Biology. From there, she pursued many creative projects, including independent films, acting, and graphic design. She has been writing since the time she could hold a pen, but launched her social media pages in April 2011. The book series, "Happiness in Your Life," is a set of twelve short books, each on a specific aspect of life but all intertwined together in many ways.

Please visit:

www.HappinessInYourLife.com

and the blog:
www.theHiYL.com

Made in the USA
Columbia, SC
02 February 2023

11529120R00088